RIVKIN'S RULES

If you wish to be successful in life choose an appropriate mentor

Nigel Littlewood

Published by
Information Australia
A.C.N. 006 042 173
75 Flinders Lane
Melbourne Vic. 3000
Telephone: (03) 9654 2800
Fax: (03) 9650 5261
Internet: www.infoaust.com
Email: mail@infoaust.com

The National Library of Australia
Cataloguing-in-Publication entry:

Rivkin, Rene.
Rivkin's rules.

ISBN 1 86350 264 5

1. Quality of life. 2. Investments. I. Littlewood, Nigel.
II. Title

332.6

Cover & Page Design: Ben Graham
Front Cover Photo: Julian Kingma/courtesy of The Age

Printed and bound in Australia by Australian Print Group

Acknowledgments

I would like to express my appreciation to the following people for their invaluable help in the creation of this book: Jordan Rivkin, Terri Sissian, Therese Leuver and of course, Rene Rivkin.

Thank you to those special people in my life who I know I could trust at the other end of a climbing rope.

Table of Contents

Introduction

A foreign visitor to Sydney once asked me, "Who is the fat guy with the cigar holding council in the corner, surrounded by people?". I searched for an appropriate description and replied, "He is my business partner, friend and mentor. He is wise, prosperous and benevolent and those around him respect, revere and often love him". Although there was more than a hint of humour in my answer, it was accurate. He was, of course, Rene Rivkin.

Most Australians know Rene as a high-profile, cigar-chomping, worry-bead-twirling, bigger-than-life, super-rich stockbroker. The press has largely chosen this profile and created this phenomenon. That is not to say that Rene does not deserve the "eccentric, flamboyant, stockmarket guru" title that the press has created, or his widespread recognition. He probably does deserve it and has never discouraged publicity (although despite popular belief, he does not actively seek it).

Despite the allure and fascination of Rene's image, after fourteen years of working with him I believe the reality is even more interesting than the press-filtered version.

There is an integrity and depth behind the public figure that, unfortunately, few people have the privilege of seeing.

Rene has a remarkable outlook on life that is often summarised by his very logical and astute one-line observations of people and events. The object of this book is to give an insight into Rene's perception of the world, the markets and people.

I have endeavoured to provide you with a collection of Rene's rules that have led him to great financial success. Rene's financial success is well known and documented, but his success in his personal life is equally impressive. He enjoys a loving marriage with his wife Gayle, to whom he has been married for twenty-five years. They have raised five beautiful children, four boys and a girl. Rene's love of children is very evident whenever there are children around. His favourite charity is the Children's Hospital, which enjoys enormous support from Rene and other great Australians. I recently watched Rene study his one-year-old god son, who was exploring his own pram, and was surprised by Rene's genuine interest and enthusiasm in the child's fascination. Rene has an amazing capacity for curiosity, and family friends have told me that he has had this since he was a child, always encouraged by his parents to ask, "Why is it so?"

One thing you should expect with Rene is to be surprised. His ability to create exciting moments is a gift that attracts people to him and ensures that life *in the family* is never dull. After fourteen years, I can vouch for that.

I have intentionally neglected interpreting each of Rene's rules. Some rules may seem a little esoteric but I believe some reflection will yield the correct message. Additionally, by not giving my own interpretation, I hope you may extract even more from his lessons in areas that apply specifically to you.

Some of Rene's rules are his exact quotes and some are observations of mine, based on how he lives.

I hope you enjoy and benefit by reading Rene's Rules. I have found that even after fourteen years, Rene continues to play the role of wise mentor and teacher to me.

The Rules on Investment

Devotion is the sweetness in life.

There is nothing that cannot happen in the markets.

All booms must bust! The only question is when.

When taxi drivers give you tips, it is time to believe the bull market is nearing its end.

Look at the downside of any transaction first. If acceptable, then examine the upside.

Missing a stockmarket winner is not a sin - but losing money is.

Never risk your lifestyle on any one investment.

The pain of losing money is greater than the pleasure of making money.

Look for low-risk trades; they are always around.

Buy in gloom, sell in boom.

Make sure you understand every investment you make. Therefore, don't invest in anything that you do not understand.

Follow the trend.

When in doubt, get out.

When a market makes a new high for the first time in a while, it will most likely continue the trend.

If you don't have a number of good reasons for holding an investment, then you should not hold it...the fact that you bought it above the current price is not a good reason.

Never underestimate the importance of patience or luck.

People wait for stockmarkets, stockmarkets do not wait for people.

There are times when preserving capital is the prime objective.

Most trading problems come from breaking one rule...cut your losses short and run your profits.

Read every bit of financial material you can lay your hands on; you never know where you will find a useful snippet.

Never spend your profits before you have liquidated the position.

Unless human behaviour changes, fear, greed and folly will always drive markets (but of course it won't).

Invest in the fundamentals, but trade the price action.

I have never met a rich chartist.

Index funds are another way of saying that you don't know what you are doing.

Investing is often about whom you know and not what you know.

Follow the winners in any field of endeavour.

Never do business with people with a shady past - no exceptions!

Don't gamble.

Consider the quality of management before the apparent fundamentals.

Never invest in stocks that are run by management that has failed in the past.

There are many valuable investment tools but few capable tradesmen to use them.

Economists' forecasts are good for one thing - to know what will not happen.

My favourite forecasters are those who are always wrong. At least they are consistent and therefore useful.

Don't waste time worrying about past mistakes - learn from them.

If a wrong decision was made based on sound evidence, there is no lesson to be learnt.

All investments are a risk proposition.

Accept the fact that investing cannot have a 100% success rate.

There is no room in trading for fear, greed, or regret.

If you are in a losing trade and it gives you an opportunity to exit and break even, it is almost always the correct action to take.

While most people in the market are optimists or pessimists, I believe there is only one sensible position: realist.

Never panic in the stockmarket.

Be passionate about stockmarket investment - it is great fun.

If something does not make sense to you, it is probably wrong.

The market spends much of its time focused on rumours.

It is very rare that the first price in a takeover bid is the last takeover price.

You will never pick the top or the bottom.

Always leave some for the next guy.

If you are happy with the quantum of profit in any investment, then take it.

Never be afraid of a small loss. It often avoids a big one.

Understand the benefits of compound interest, dollar cost averaging and forced savings.

The higher the real NTA (net tangible asset backing), the lower the risk.

Be wary of investment in start-ups.

High-growth stocks should not have a high dividend payout ratio.

Put more emphasis on historical earnings than future earnings forecasts.

Look for companies with a consistently high return on capital.

You can make money in bull or bear stockmarkets.

If you are in doubt about the prospects for any particular industry, consult an expert in that industry.

It is easier to not find oil than to find oil.

Derivatives trading is for experts only.

Insider trading is illegal.
'Insighter' trading is highly legal.

The value of insider trading is also over-rated, as Warren Buffett says: "With enough inside information and a million dollars, you can go broke in a year".

Nurture your insight. Aspire to be a good insighter trader.

Have a set of rules that you must follow.

The hardest rule to follow is the previous one.

Almost all my losses have been because I strayed from my investment rules.

Keep your set of rules simple.

Investment is part science and part art. Therefore, I can't answer all the questions. Some queries are best solved by close and individual study of the market's price action. And some problems will never be solved.

Rene on Success

"I love my boat. It gets used almost everyday.
I do most of my business on board." - Rene Rivkin.

There is only one test of success and that is happiness.

If you wish to enjoy life, treat money as a replaceable resource.

Power is measured by the ability to influence people's feelings.

It is better to be unhappy and rich than unhappy and poor.

Do whatever it takes to make you happy, as long as it hurts no one else.

Reward loyalty.

Focus on the positives.

Hire people to do the jobs that you can't, or don't want to do.

Know who you are.

Find a mentor.

No person has ever been successful without the help of somebody else.

If you wish to stay excited about life, don't stop learning.

In life, stick to what you are good at.

Associate with successful people because some of it is bound to rub off. I always have.

There is no such thing as a get-rich-quick scheme. When it does happen, it is pure luck. Don't forget that.

Do not compromise your integrity.

There is a cost for living in the greatest country in the world, but don't pay more tax than you are legally required to.

You can't be liked by everybody.

Management consultants amaze me, they tell you how to get rich but they fail to get rich.

You do not have to be ruthless to be successful. But you do, to be a billionaire.

Never give up on the pursuit of your goals.

Rene on Sex and Relationships

*A classic family portrait. From left: Shannon,
Gayle, Rene & Tara, Dion (seated), Damien and Jordan.*

Don't expect the opposite sex to be rational.

Fat and unfit people aren't as good in bed as fit people.

Have lots of children...if you can afford them.

A partnership should make sense.

Decide what you want from a relationship.

Tell your partner you love them every day.

The more I shit-stir you, the more I like you.

Love as you want to be loved.

Be generous.

Challenge your loved ones.

Having no relationship is better than having a bad one.

Unfortunately, looks are important but beauty is in the eye of the beholder.

Don't let life get boring if you can avoid it.

Believe whatever makes you happy but don't impose your beliefs on others.

A partnership of two high-libido people is less likely to last than that of two low-libido people.

No relationship can exist without a great deal of compromise.

Sex and love are definitely not the same thing.

Have time apart from your partner, as absence definitely makes the heart grow fonder.

Nurture the relationship with your spouse. Don't forget that when the children leave, they are all you have left to live with.

Each member of a partnership must have his or her own space.

Never expect perfection in a marriage. It almost never exists.

Men and women are designed to be together, but not to live together forever.

Rene on Life

Rene entertaining the Baywatch team. He had a cameo role (playing himself) in one Sydney filmed episode.

Live with passion.

Unless God is omnipotent, omniscient and benevolent, I am not interested. Therefore, there is no God.

If heaven is as good as its marketing suggests, how come nobody wants to get there quickly?

If you are not happy, take a risk and make changes.

Be curious and ask, "Why is it so?"

Associate with people who make you happy.

Don't believe what you hear or read in the press. I know, because only 50% of what is written about me is correct.

As long as it doesn't hurt others, do what you want to do.

Apart from professional sports people, sport is counter-productive to making money.

I am unfit because I do not do sport. Nigel is unfit because he does.

I always try to surround myself with beauty - women, men, art and nature. It is very important to me.

Make life easier if you can.

Reading fiction is for fun, there is no financial benefit.

Health is all-important.

In life, not every bargain is a bargain.

Enjoy this life. It is not a trial run.

I don't hate anyone. Hatred is totally counter-productive.

Don't panic or stress. It does not help.

There is a big difference between being spoiled and being spoilt.

Life does not punish evil or reward goodness enough.

Rene on Politics

If you are a politician, you must sometimes lie. Just accept it.

Individuals can only have a major impact by accident.

Political power is largely illusory; all power is largely illusory. Consider the world's most powerful man, Bill Clinton. He did not have the power to stop an investigation into his sexual pleasure.

Economic prosperity has far more to do with economic cycles than good political policy.

There is no better place to be poor than in Australia.

Many people believe politicians should be paid more. I believe it would change nothing.

Rene's Favourite Rivkinisms

"If you like it, buy it."

There is nothing quite like a good laugh.

I like accommodating people.

If you don't like it here, leave!

You can do whatever you want, as long as you don't hurt other people.

Thankfully, I am just a big kid afterall.

I started smoking cigars because I liked them, now they are my trademark and I have to smoke them whether I want to or not.

I love cars because they are sculptures on wheels. And how can I have too many sculptures?

My worry bead habit started in 1973. I took them up to give up cigarettes and they worked, until I got a brain tumour in 1987 when I thought I was going to die.

The press calls me flamboyant. I don't know exactly what that is, but it seems to have helped my career so I am prepared to accept the term. I would agree that I am eccentric, as I am unquestionably different to most people.

I have no doubt that Australia is the greatest country in the world to live in.

The author at work.

About the Author

The most difficult challenges provide the greatest rewards.

Devotion is the sweetness in life.

I was born on the 10th of October, 1966 in Sydney, Australia. My father was a naval officer and my mother a teacher. As a child, I was moved around the world with my family, finally settling in Sydney when I was 16 years old. I had always wanted to live in Sydney and was very fortunate to finish my high school years on (an all-round) scholarship at Bellevue Hill's Cranbrook School. It was an excellent school that nurtured and encouraged the development of individuals and not clones. I made many friends there who are still in my life today.

At the end of my formal education, I can only describe myself as an excellent all-rounder. I was not great at anything but I was quite good at everything except music and art. So, armed with my commonsense, good sporting and communication skills and an acceptable brain, I deferred university for a year to work and travel in Europe.

On my return home in 1986, I was convinced that being poor was not for me. Travelling through Europe for three months on $8 a day and living on the poverty line in London for another nine months had guaranteed that.

In mid-1986, I became a stockmarket chalkie on the Sydney Stock Exchange. It had never made sense for me to attend university and learn a whole heap of useless information that would never bring me either pleasure or financial gain. At least that was my attitude at the time.

I was not impassioned by any particular profession such as medicine or law, so I entered the exciting world of shares during one of the greatest booms of all time. My family had never had much money and had convinced me that we had even less. My mother and father were brought up by parents who had lived through the Great Depression and who practiced the art of frugality to the point of obsession. My parents brought me up the same way. The one thing that I was sure about was that I did not ever want to worry about money. So I went to work where all the money was, hoping to get enough for myself.

Everybody in the market was making obscene amounts of money in that boom and thought that it would always be that way.

I was sitting on the lowest rung on the ladder, but I was excited and optimistic about the future. By being on the trading floor, a chalkie is immersed in the action and gets to play a humble but critical role in the whole show. By being in the heart of all the activity, my ambition was ignited even further.

One of the most important things in life is to feel that your objectives are achievable. When I was a chalkie, I could see and smell the money every day and watch Rene Rivkin ruling over the market like Michael Jordan on a basketball court. My objectives were very clear to me. Make a prosperous future for myself and my family in the stockmarket by serving Rene Rivkin. It did not make sense to work for anybody else because he was the undisputed best in his field and that is where the best chance of success lay.

The fact that he did not know me was a minor hurdle but one I was determined to overcome. I read *Going for it* by Victor Kiam and, armed with a number of strategies, approached the big man for a job. The optimism of innocence is a beautiful thing at that age. I felt about three feet tall on the trading floor asking him for the opportunity to convince him that he could not survive in business without my invaluable support.

He was amused by my bold approach and granted me a meeting first thing the next morning.

Courtesy of some inside information, I arrived at Rene's office at about the same time he did, at 7am. It was a large and imposing office with papers everywhere, an enormous coffee jug and a bank of phones on the huge, dark-timber desk. This was pretty scary stuff for a twenty-year-old upstart who suddenly realised Rene Rivkin had probably forgotten more about the stockmarket than I was ever likely to know in my entire life.

Fortunately, Rene generally goes relatively easy on people when he first meets them. It is only after a number of years that the quizzing, teasing and shit-stirring really get going into full swing. His first question was the same for all young hopefuls wanting to work for him. "Do you like money?" There is only one correct answer. You would not want to fail at this early point.

We got on very well, which we both acknowledged. Unfortunately, there was a problem. Rene did not need more trading floor staff. Courtesy of his habit of hiring friends' offspring as favours, Rivkin James Capel was overstaffed with many inefficient employees. I needed an ace to play, so I offered to work for nothing until Rene offered me a job. I was to get my first Rivkin investment lesson. "I can't refuse a trade with no downside," he smiled. I had my chance.

About two weeks later, I had the dream job I wanted, and the start of an adventurous career.

I was fortunate enough to join the inner team that had access to Rene and had the benefit of working with him every day. Late one evening in mid-1987, not long after I started with Rivkin James Capel, Rene and I were sitting in his huge, dark office working on an administration problem at nine o'clock at night. In those days, Rene and I regularly worked twelve-hour days and I was being paid $12,000 a year.

Neither Rene nor I should have been working on such an issue but due to an archaic settlement system and an inexperienced back office, Rene and I sometimes found ourselves dealing with these sorts of inconveniences. I was amazed that Rene was wasting precious time and energy on such basic management issues. I felt that this huge bureaucracy that had developed around him was eroding his contribution to this company and I told him. I shared my view that he was being handicapped by having this enormous stockbroking organisation that stopped him focusing on what he did best. In those days, Rene was broker to many of Australia's high fliers. Businessmen like Alan Bond and Kerry Packer were on the phone daily to speak to The Boss and get his market advice. (In those days we called him The Boss). I was amazed that he and I were sitting at his desk discussing some script problem from two months ago. After telling him of my new micro Rivkin broking firm, he agreed with my view and confirmed that it was soon to proceed. I will never forget what he said next: "And you will be part of it". Well, that was the biggest honour I could have received. Despite the wealth that I have accumulated due to my association with Rene Rivkin, I have always got more satisfaction from gaining Rene's respect.

In late 1988, a year after the infamous stockmarket crash, I decided the bear market was going to be around for awhile. I took two years off to live and work in Canada. I spent two years pretending to be a Canadian working in the famous Whistler restaurant, The Rim Rock Café. I spent every day skiing and racked up 100 days on the snow in my first year in Whistler. I learnt to be a ski instructor and kid's racing coach while becoming an expert spectator in ice hockey and baseball. The regular Tuesday trip to Vancouver with my Whistler buddies to watch ice hockey and visit the casinos became legendary. I fell in love with British Columbia and still have many friends back there.

I always thought that I would have to grow up and return home someday. Well, I returned home. I figured I could defer growing up a bit longer.

I came back to Australia at the start of 1991. Later that year, Rene decided to close down Rivkin and Co to retire. Rene missed the trading floor. His skills did not immediately adapt to trading on the new computerised SEATS (stock exchange automated trading system) screens. Not only that, but the recession of the early 1990s left the stockmarket, as Rene once said, "as lifeless as Rookwood cemetery".

When Rene retired, I went to work at Bell securities as a private client broker and then moved to SBC Australia (the Australian arm of the large Swiss banking group) to work as an institutional advisor.

While I loved working in the stockmarket, I never felt comfortable on a dealing desk. I felt that I was selling somebody else's product that I did not really believe in or fully understand. I also never felt at home in the aggressive, corporate environment that prevailed in the dealing room of SBC.

In late 1995, about two years after I started with SBC, it merged with Warburgs. I was relieved to accept a retrenchment and said my final goodbyes to a career that had paid me well and taught me a lot, but which I hated. I had remained friendly with Rene through my post-Rivkin stockmarket career but there was no plan at this stage to join forces again. He was happily retired and spent his time investing in the market, coffee shop hopping and building a world-class car collection.

In 1996, I became a semi-full-time sailor, racing 18ft skiffs, and then a full-time futures trader.

That year was probably the most self-exposing and strengthening year of my life. I decided to become a full-time futures trader and proceeded to make every mistake that most beginner traders make. My inability to take a quick loss peaked in mid-1996 when I finally realised a $40,000 loss on one trade.

I had not been educated in an environment that taught me to accept mistakes, congratulate myself for learning so much and realise what a valuable lesson I had just been blessed with. My reaction to my failure was sheer depression and self-doubt. I remember sitting watching the ocean from my window, feeling like a complete loser. I dug as deep as I could to find the strength that would enable me to make the right decision as to what my next move should be. I was so disorientated by the loss that I was struggling to make a decision about what to have for lunch, let alone what to do with my trading career. After many tears and soul searching, I made the call. I never give up! And I didn't. I focused on my weaknesses and set about developing a trading system that avoided my weaknesses having a derogatory influence on my trading. My results started improving immediately.

That moment of truth changed my attitude towards almost everything. My good buddy James Craigie and I once climbed Mt Aspiring in New Zealand. We discovered strengths that we had never seen before in ourselves. Most of us don't know what we are capable of because we never get tested. That is why I like climbing because you test your limits, and find out what you really have inside. It is usually a pleasant surprise.

Through that very tough time I learnt one very powerful lesson. Failure is an inevitable part of success. As children we are taught to fear and avoid failure. All successful people that I know have learnt to accept the inevitable failures that accompany the path to great success. They learn from them and move on. I often wonder how much better Australia would be if we encouraged people to push the limits and accept the failures, rather than take the safe option.

Towards the end of 1996, Rene came to me with the idea of a stockmarket newsletter. The idea sparked an energy in me. I found a new lease on life and threw myself into building a publishing business called *The Rene Rivkin Report*. I did not know anything about publishing but how hard could it be? My fear of failure had miraculously disappeared and the thought of building my own business ignited my ambition like never before. Hire good consultants was my number one rule and it worked.

It is now fourteen years after I approached Rene Rivkin for a $12,000-a-year phone clerk job. Today I call him "family". I do not know exactly what my life would be like without him. I am sure he would be depressed, penniless and desperate without my loyal support... Well, perhaps not penniless.

I have benefited enormously from his moral as well as professional guidance. He has helped me become who I am and has helped me like myself (a valuable gift). As a mentor, I could hope for no better.

Despite areas that we will always disagree on, such as my mountain climbing and love of outdoor adventuring, my success is evidence of the relevance of Rene Rivkin's rules for success in life and investment, as my life strategy is largely based on them.

I truly hope you enjoy reading Rene's rules and that they help you improve your life.

Never forget that life is a journey and not a destination. Perfection is what we aspire to but what we achieve is what we must be happy with.